Get Back Up...and Do It Again!

Key Principles for Transforming Your
Life from the Inside Out

Nicole Moore Waddell

Best Life On Purpose Now

DEDICATION

I dedicate this book to my parents who have always encouraged and supported me through the ups and downs of my life, my Mommy and Daddy (Sheila and Michael). I also thank God for entrusting me with two sons (Omari & Isaiah) who are my anchor and reason to *Get Back Up...and Do It Again*!

In loving memory of my best friend, confidant, and cheerleader, my granddaddy Abraham (Abe) Moore

CONTENTS

INTRODUCTION

"Be the change you want to see in the World."
Mahatma Gandhi

As I approach Las Vegas, Nevada I see hundreds of miles of land masses with peaks and valleys. It seems as if it goes on forever with no sight of human life. Then suddenly, in the middle of nowhere, appears a narrow body of water. As I continue to look out the window of the plane I realize that life is synonymous to the desert plains of Nevada. Oftentimes, we go from day to day experiencing dryness or routine that leaves us with a sense that nothing seems to change. We become stuck in a rut like the hamster on his wheel going around and around with no real destination in sight.

We experience the peaks and valleys of life along our journey. But, just like those continuous land masses in Nevada, suddenly a body of water pops up to quench the yearning that we each have for something new. The question is will you allow the water to flow by you or will you stop and take a drink or even better will you jump in and allow your life to be refreshed for something new, something better, something purposeful?

As I write this book, I am reminded of the numerous projects that I started and stopped; the ideas that never got implemented; and the dreams that never came true. And, I ask the question: why? Why have so many opportunities slipped right through my hands? The answer: I allowed it. Yes, I allowed the fear of the unknown, procrastination, lack of follow-through, denial, betrayal, and worst of all, simple laziness keep me from fulfilling the dreams and passions that tap my very soul.

Now, don't get me wrong, I was fortunate enough to own a somewhat successful consulting business for several years. However, I allowed the disappointment of lost contracts, uncommitted staff, closed doors, and most of all a lack of dedication to keep me from reaching higher levels in my business. I decided to take the easy way out and get a "9 to 5" job instead of continuing to pursue my business. I decided to become "status quo," which led me down a path that did not reflect my God-given purpose in life. Now, before you judge me, ask yourself the question: *Am I doing what I was born to do or what I know to do for now (in the moment)?*

I can only speak for myself that I know God created me for more than just "this." What is "this" you ask? "This" is playing it safe. "This" is settling for less than you deserve. "This" is performing at a lower capacity or level of quality than you are capable of. "This" is choosing Mr. or Ms. Right Now over Mr. or Ms. Right. "This" is choosing a boring and agonizing steady W-2 pay check with benefits over the benefit of the freedom of owning your own business and making decisions for yourself that lead to unlimited revenue and income. "This" is choosing over "that" which brings you joy, peace, love, happiness, hope, faith, and a life of expecting the unexpected.

As I am in the midst of writing this book, I am facing various obstacles, of which many are self-imposed. The obstacles are attempting to keep me pigeon-holed and paralyzed from completing my God-given assignment of writing this book. In the last 12 months, I have experienced the death of two grandparents; a rocky relationship; a setback in my career; and a pervading sense of loss. But, I am determined that each of these experiences are opportunities to learn, improve, and propel me into my destiny.

A life of expecting is a life of believing that where you are going is better than where you are right now. This book explores key principles for making the necessary changes in your life that will move you beyond where you are today and to take the action steps necessary to go forward in life. After years of living below my potential, I have finally made the decision to ***Get Back Up…and Do It Again!***

Chapter 1

WHAT YOU SEE IS NOT WHAT YOU GET...BUT WHAT YOU CHOOSE TO DO IS

"If you can't fly, then run, if you can't run, then walk, if you can't walk, then crawl, but whatever you do you have to keep moving forward."
Dr. Martin Luther King, Jr.

Every day we are faced with decisions and choices. Do we choose to move forward or backward? What drives us to choose one option over another? Often we are driven by emotions. We can choose based on fear or anticipation of something new and exciting. Our ability to choose begins with our attitude toward the situation. We can choose to look at the glass half-empty or half-full. You've heard it said that our attitude determines our altitude. We achieve the next level in life or overcome the present challenges by choosing to walk by faith and not by sight. We grow into new and exciting areas of life when we live with expectation that something great is going to happen to us TODAY.

I used to be that person who second-guessed whether certain situations or relationships could actually be for me. It seemed too good to be true. I would self-sabotage the moment or opportunity. I would tell myself, *He has to be hiding something* or *this opportunity is only going to last for a brief moment, so don't get attached.*

I found myself straddling the fence between faith and doubt. We know that faith and doubt cannot operate in the same space. One will overtake the other. One is an offensive move (faith) and another is a defensive move (doubt).

Just like in the game of sports, it is the offense that scores the points and changes the score. It is time for you to change the scoreboard of your life. If the offensive line focused on just what they saw in front of them, they would never push beyond the 300lb plus lineman and defensive backs. A truly successful professional athlete plays with heart, thus choosing to believe that they are invisible and can combat the tackle of their opponent. That is just how life is.

"You see that his faith and his actions were working together, and his faith was made complete by what he did. " James 2:22 NIV

As stated in the book of James, your faith has to be paired with action in order to obtain what you hope for in life. We cannot simply lie around wishing for things to happen. We must walk out our faith one step at a time. What is it that you are hoping for? What step can you take right now to back up what you are hoping for? Remember our faith is not in our ability to make things happen, but our faith in the promise that we can do all things through Christ (Philippians 4:13).

We live day-to-day doing our daily grind (routine) and then suddenly an obstacle comes along. You are laid off or your spouse wants a divorce. You have been diagnosed with cancer or your child decides to raise all the hell they can muster up. Nevertheless, it is not the situation that knocks us out or puts us on the sidelines of life. Rather, it is our reaction to the situation. Are you going to see this obstacle as a life-altering disaster or as an opportunity to embrace and initiate effective change in your life?

Our choice to move forward or to stay paralyzed in our emotional state of disappointment or despair is simply a decision! You decide if you want to be happy or depressed, joyful or miserable, mad or sad; it is all up to you. Are you going to go through life affected by what happens to you or are you going to affect the outcomes?

This day choose life or death. Remember that the power of life and death is in the tongue. Speak in faith according to God's positive promises, not in the negative. God has good plans and a bright future for each of us. Declare over your mind and spirit what God says about the awesome plans he has for you.

"For I know the plans I have for you, "declares the Lord, "plans to prosper you and not to harm you, plans to give you hope and a future." Jeremiah 29:11

What do you choose for yourself today? Are you focusing on what is missing or lacking in your life? Or do you see by faith new beginnings, a fresh start, and better ideas?

Change is not an option, but a decision. A decision to do something you have never done in order to experience something you never have before. Choices decide decisions and decisions dictate what we get out of life. Changes come in many forms. Sometimes it is a change in relationships, while other times it is a change in a job or physical location of your home.

> **Changes + Choices =**
> *Elevation to Your*
> *Life's Destiny*

Whatever the change may be, your decision to embrace or abandon the changes will have an impact on the future outcomes of your life. I frequently remind my sons that for every decision -- good or bad -- we make in life, there are consequences -- good or bad. A choice to assess and implement changes in your life directly impacts your future and the path that it takes along the journey.

Changes occur in life to make us stronger and more aware of God's power in us and through us. I had to learn through my own journey that I could not always react to how things appeared to be. I had to embrace the promise that my choices required steps of faith without any available facts. I learned that sometimes God requires me to move forward without having all of my ducks in a row.

"Now faith is the substance of things hoped for, the evidence of things not seen." Hebrews 11:1 KJV

Now is the time to reach your destiny. That means making the choice to move forward without having all the pieces to the puzzle. I have often said to friends that if we knew every step of what God had intended for us, we would ruin His ultimate goal for our lives because our human nature is to step in and control things. The sooner we realize that God is the Alpha and Omega, the sooner we can experience the purpose and plans He has for our lives.

"I am Alpha and Omega, the beginning and the ending, says the Lord, which is, and which was, and which is to come, the Almighty." Revelations 1:8 KJV

We don't have to worry about what tomorrow holds, because God knows the beginning from the end. We just have to trust that what He has begun, He is faithful to fulfill. Trust is a firm belief that God is reliable, capable, and able to bring to pass what He has directed you to do. Make today the first day that you will make the decision to take the next step to your destiny. The choice is up to you.

Chapter 5 of this book will further define and outline how to embrace change as a positive force in your life.

Chapter 2

FEAR IS NOT AN OPTION

"I learned that courage was not the absence of fear, but the triumph over it. The brave man is not he who does not feel afraid, but he who conquers that fear."
Nelson Mandela

God does not give us the spirit of fear, but of power, love, and a sound mind. I remember the day I decided that I was going to turn in my resignation from what some would consider a good government job. I had taken a two-year hiatus from my consulting business to take what I thought was a temporary role within the State government. Three roles and two years later I found myself in a place in which I was asking myself how I got there.

It was not the first time I asked myself this question, but for some reason it had a more piercing effect on me.

I had become complacent and frankly feared going back out on my own as an independent contractor. But, I knew God was directing me to make a change. Even though I had complained over the last year about the environment, I continued to press ahead in the day-to-day routine of my tasks. In my heart I knew God had more in store for me and I wanted more. However, I let the fear of the unknown and the fear of failure paralyze me from moving ahead. I was reminded that fear has in the past been defined as **False Evidence Appearing Real**. So, let's examine this for a moment.

False
Evidence
Appearing
Real

Over my lifetime I have feared most of all what others would think if I decided to make certain changes in my life. I have come to realize slowly, but surely, that it is more important to be a God Pleaser vs. a People Pleaser. When I was younger, change was exciting because I always looked forward to the unknown. As I have gotten older and have taken on the responsibility of motherhood, I find that my desire to change is more calculated and not as risk-taking as it was in my 20s and early 30s.

I question more of what the impact of my desire to change has on me, my family, and my overall environment. At first I thought this meant that I was denying change, but now I understand that analyzing the impact of change can be equated to a level of maturity and growth in wisdom. However, delayed change over time due to fear and excuses, just simply becomes denial of one's true self.

Let's think about this for a moment. The word false speaks of something that *is not* true. Evidence is proof of something. Appearing is being or what you see with the naked eye. The word "real" denotes something is authentic. So in other words, fear is proof of something being not true.

So, if what appears to be natural, really in fact is NOT what is being manifested in the spirit, what is stopping us from making the changes we need to make in our life? Where does this false evidence appearing real come from? Where else? Our mind! Most of us have heard the saying, *mind over matter*, but what does that really mean? How many times have you been somewhere or tried to have a conversation with someone and your mind kept racing with a million things you had to do?

> *Fear is proof of something being not true.*

The fact of the matter is that the presence of fear is the absence of faith. The absence of believing that what God has promised you will come to pass. Fear is the absence of assurance that nothing is impossible with God. The presence of fear paralyzes many of us in our tracks.

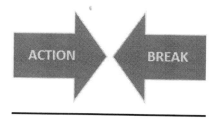

ACTION BREAK

- ❖ What fears are you facing today?
- ❖ What is the source of this fear?
- ❖ What is the worst thing that could happen if you made a decision to do things differently?

We manifest much of our fear through contemplating the unknown. Trying to determine the *what-ifs* can be exhausting and fruitless. We must learn how to overcome fear by trusting what God has for us *is for us*. We must make a decision that whatever the next second, minute, day, or year to come brings, we have the power to change our perspective about the future.

"Trust in the Lord with all of your heart and lean not to your own understanding and He (God) will direct your path." Proverbs 3:5-6 NIV

Exercise faith to believe that God wants the best for you no matter how your current situation appears. I know you are probably saying to yourself *"you don't know my situation."* And you are right. But, what I do know is that there is nothing new under the sun. Someone somewhere has experienced the trials, tribulations, and triumphs you have experienced. The difference is perspective.

I have learned over time that when I make the decision to own my plight in life and see it as a learning experience instead of a punishment, I have peace in the situation. This takes courage and determination to face my fears with the faith that God promised never to leave me or forsake me.

Experiencing faith takes practice. Just like building your biceps or developing those 6-pack abs, it takes *Focus, Action, Intention, Tenacity,* and *Humility.*

Focus entails paying attention in order to see clearly.

Action requires you to do something in order to achieve a goal or dream. One of my all-time favorite marketing campaigns is Nike's *Just Do It.*

To live with **Intention** means that you live with and for a purpose. You set your sights on a goal and aim for it.

A person of **Tenacity** is persistent in achieving their goals and determined not to let anything or anyone distract them in reaching their dreams.

The Focus + Action + Intention + Tenacity formula for exercising faith in your life is not complete without **Humility**. Many people view **Humility** as a deficiency or weakness, but it is actually the opposite. A person of **Humility** as it relates to faith is someone who recognizes that they are reliant and dependent upon the wisdom, knowledge, and guidance from God. **Humility** is a quiet confidence in knowing that you can accomplish your dreams not because you are so great, but because God is so loving, kind, merciful, and full of grace; He empowers you to have life and live it more abundantly.

> **F**ocus
> **A**ction
> **I**nteraction
> **T**enacity
> **H**umility

"A man's mind plans his way [as he journeys through life], But the Lord directs his steps and establishes them." Proverbs 16:9 AMP

Chapter 3

GOING BEYOND THE POINT OF NOT YET

"The secret of change is to focus all of your energy, not on fighting the old, but on building the new."
Socrates

Have you ever been in a place or situation in which you are expecting something to happen, but it never to seems to come? You have been working hard, taking on more projects, stepping up at work to showcase your leadership skills, but to no avail. You do not get the promotion or the compensation you expected. I know that I can attest to this exact situation happening in my life.

It appears that the more you give, the less you receive back in recognition. At those points in time I had to remind myself that my promotion does not come from the east or the west, but from God. He is the author and the finisher of my faith. So, what does that mean? It means that if what I expected did not happen when I expected it to, I had to trust that God had a bigger plan and knew better than I what was best for me at the time. And guess what? He did know better. The project I thought I just had to lead turned out to be the project from hell. The position I thought I had to have turned out to be completely reorganized and would have brought me more stress than success. Instead, by losing out on what appeared to be a good thing, I waited and received God's best thing for me.

One of the most important lessons and challenges in life is learning to wait. The scriptures say, "But they that wait upon the Lord shall renew their strength; they shall mount up with wings as eagles; they shall run, and not be weary; and they shall walk, and not faint." Isaiah 40:31 KJV

What does it mean to "to wait"?
What do you do while you are waiting?

Waiting is defined as: *to stay where one is or delay action until a particular time or until something else happens.*

Oftentimes we confuse the word "wait" with the thought of inaction. However, there are small steps that we can take along our journey that ultimately lead us toward our goal in due season. I have discovered over time that to every season there is truly a purpose. Like a farmer, there is as a season to sow (plant and prepare) and a season to reap (harvest). You don't simply plant an apple seed today and expect to see an apple tree tomorrow with ripened fruit ready to be picked. You have to cultivate the ground, water the seed, remove the weeds, and fertilize the soil. The same is true in our everyday lives.

For example, you have been searching for a new job for over a year, but nothing seems to be happening. Did you hear what I said before? A delay is not a denial! We are disappointed because things don't happen in our timing or quite the way we expected it to. But, if you are truly honest with yourself, there are situations that you now look back on and thank God you didn't get what you asked for at the time. Perhaps it was a relationship with a man or a woman who you thought you would love forever and would never be able to live without.

> **Be encouraged...a delay is not a denial!**

As the old adage goes, *time heals all wounds.* Now of course it doesn't feel like the hurt will ever heal until one day you meet Mr. or Mrs. Right. Suddenly, you realize that what you have been crying over was never good for you. Don't get me wrong. I believe there is something to learn from every experience and relationship in life. You should never look at mistakes or bad decisions as a waste of time or the end of your life. Just take the time to reflect on your decisions and make better decisions moving forward.

Not yet can be a gift in disguise. Use the waiting period as a moment to reflect on ways to make yourself better. It may require an attitude adjustment or a new way of thinking about the circumstances in your life. Perhaps the waiting period is a chance to advance your skills in a particular area or expand your knowledge of a subject that will allow you to be more competitive when the next opportunity occurs.

We serve an awesome God who has promised that He is the same yesterday, today, and forevermore. When you put your mind and your will to work, God will reward you for all of your hard work. *Not yet* can allow you time to get into the right place at the right time to receive the right blessing for you.

"May our Lord Jesus Christ himself and God our Father, who loved us and by his grace gave us eternal encouragement and good hope, encourage your hearts and strengthen you in every good deed and word."
2 Thessalonians 2:16-17

Keep on keeping on no matter the trial or tribulation. Remember, for every *No* or *Not yet* there is a *Yes*. You just have to:

**Get Back Up...and
Do It Again!**

Chapter 4

THE ACT FACTOR

"Because the people who are crazy enough to think they can change the world are the ones who do."
Steve Jobs

When you think about beginning something new, oftentimes you feel anxious or intimidated. But, opening yourself up to new opportunities can lead you down the path of change that will impact your life in a positive manner. Meeting new people, trying new adventures, going to new places are what enable us to grow in life. I want to expand my territory beyond the limits of my finite experiences. How does one grow unless they are rooted and planted in the soil of belief and faith that each day is a day to **ACT**?

The ACT Factor

Let us explore the concept of the **ACT Factor** on a deeper level. The first element of the ACT Factor is **Attitude**. Attitude is the manner or feeling with regards to a person or thing.

Have you ever met someone who always seems to be stuck? No matter the season or circumstance, whenever you ask them how life is treating them, there is this woe-is-me answer. These are folks that we refer to as the "victim mentality" people. Their attitude is always negative and every situation is somebody else's fault. It reminds me of the man at the pool of Bethesda who told the disciples that he had no one to put him into the pool to be healed. After 30+ years of lying near the pool, he could have rolled, crawled, or simply asked someone for help. We block our ability to change and embrace the great possibilities of our future when we have a self-defeating, fearful, or entitlement attitude.

Decide today that you are going to change your attitude. Our thought-life has to be renewed daily by what we read, what we listen to on the television, and even whose advice we take. Your attitude determines your altitude.

"For as he thinks in his heart, so is he..."
Proverbs 23:7a AMP

How high or how far do you want your life to go? For some, the next level is finding that special someone with whom to spend the rest of your life. For others, it is climbing the corporate ladder, while for yet others it is literally the dream of climbing Mt. Everest. Whatever the next thing may be, it is how you think or envision your ability to achieve that goal that greatly impacts and determines your ability to do it.

Your attitude requires a certain level of **Courage,** the second element of the **ACT Factor** that needs to be considered. Courage is the ability to do something that frightens you. A person's success does not mean there was an absence of fear. Most successful people invoke courage to see their dream manifest.

The third element in the ACT Factor is **Trust**. To trust is the belief that someone or something is reliable, good, honest, or effective. Trust is an assured reliance that what you are believing to happen will indeed come to pass. We have to learn how to trust ourselves, as well as others. Now this is not blindsided trust, but trust that is based on wisdom and experience. The first step in developing trust is trusting God's ability to do what He has promised.

"You need to persevere so that when you have done the will of God, you will receive what he has promised." Hebrews 10:36 NIV

The transformational principles outlined in this book require you to go beyond your normal day to day life.

The **ACT Factor** leads to achievement. To achieve means to obtain or successfully complete a goal. This goal could be maintaining a healthy lifestyle, starting a business, or establishing a loving relationship. Whatever the goal may be, in order to achieve it you must purpose in your mind that you will take the actions necessary to fulfill it.

Does it mean you will not have fear of failure or you will not make a mistake along the way? Of course not! But, many of us never achieve our goals in life because we let both external forces and our internal negative conversations keep us from moving forward.

The only thing that really hinders us from reaching our goals is simply a decision. Yes, a simple decision not to go through the process is what keeps us from achieving our goals. Decide today to move forward and take action. *Get Back Up…and Do It Again*.

Chapter 5

CHANGE MAKES THE WORLD GO ROUND

"Change will not come if we wait for some other person or some other time. We are the ones we've been waiting for. We are the change that we seek."
President Barack H. Obama

What Is Change?

Change is an alteration of the current state of affairs that impacts the current situation either positively or negatively. Change requires you to step out of your comfort zone and into the unknown to seek new ways of doing things.

Change can be either temporary or permanent. Change challenges you to look deep within to ascertain what is important to you and your development as a person. When you decide to change or accept change it affects everyone connected to you. Others are not always receptive to your need or desire to change. This lack of support will oftentimes paralyze people from pursuing the passion for change.

"The one thing we can depend on besides death and taxes...is change."

Who Is Affected By Change?

No one is exempt from change. Even as a baby, you experience the change of transitioning from crawling to walking. As a teenage boy you experience the change in his voice...squeak to bass. As a young adult you evolve from being dependent when living with your parents to becoming independent when you move out on your own.

Questions about Change

❖ What is change?
❖ Who is affected by change?
❖ Why don't people like to change?
❖ What is the impact of change?
❖ What is the impact of not changing?
❖ How can I balance change in my life?

Fleeing the Fear of Change

What is it about change that we fear so much? Is it the fear of failure or the fear of success? Do we fear what others will think about our new idea or outlook on life? Are we fearful of the potential cost of change? So, what does change cost?

Sometimes change costs us the loss of a relationship. Perhaps, relocation from an environment you have grown to accept (not necessarily like). Change may cost you your reputation. But, you must ask yourself if the benefit of the change outweighs the cost.

Oftentimes we try to talk ourselves out of change. *"Oh, I can't change because...*

❖ *I am too old.*
❖ *I am not smart enough.*
❖ *I like me just the way I am.*

Just imagine for once or even better...say for once the opposite:

❖ *I can change because I am mature enough.*
❖ *I can change because I have education/ wisdom.*
❖ *I want to change because I want to be a better person.*

Seasons of Change

Just as seasons must change, so must our lives. Seasons are transitions from one experience to the next or from one level to the next. Seasons come and go. Some seasons repeat themselves just as they did the year(s) before; while other seasons bring unexpected changes that are not normal or unusual for that particular season. So even though we depend upon some sense of predictability within each season, there is always the element of the unknown and the unplanned.

Let's examine for a moment the changes that occur in life's seasons.

•**Winter "Season of Decision"**: The beginning of the year is signified by what some would describe as a season of "deadness." The night air is crisp and brisk, the trees are barren, and the grass is dry and brittle. Much of the earth's habitat hibernates during this season for safety and shelter. Life is filled with new beginnings. Winter is a time to reflect on your successes and failures in order to prepare for the new season of opportunities. The still of winter enables you to make decisions and plans for achieving the goals you want to accomplish. This season is necessary to prepare for the future. It is during winter that you press into the wisdom and understanding of God's purpose and divine destiny for you.

•Spring "Season of Growth": A season marked by new beginnings. The rain falls to quench the earth. The trees and the flowers bud. The grass grows and turns green. The birds sing and the earth's habitat begins to resurface from hibernation. The days of sunlight become longer. The seeds (prayers, plans, expectations) you plant in the winter begin to come to fruition. Your thoughts and ideas in conjunction with your plans bring you into alignment with your purpose.

•Summer "Season of Prosperity":
Revitalization throughout the earth is seen and felt. Flowers bloom in abundance. The sun's rays warm the earth; animals produce new life. The life's surface is restored. Your purpose takes on meaning and affects the lives around you. God's divine order for your life manifests itself from the spirit into the natural.

•Fall "Season of Preparation/ Sustenance": the heat of the summer is replaced with cool nights. Trees provide a display of vibrant color. The earth's habitat hunt and store for sustainment. Even though the seasons continue to change, your God given purpose remains. Your purpose evolves as you grow and develop; and takes on new shape in order to impact even more lives for the kingdom of God and His glory.

We are always tempted to tell others what, how, and why they need to change, but fail to measure ourselves along the same standards.

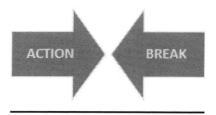

Remember…the only person you can change is **YOU!!!** Take a few moments and think about one major area in your life that needs to change.

1. Why do you fear change in this area?
2. What obstacles have you told yourself are barriers to changing in this area?
3. For each obstacle list a fear buster – Action Plan.
4. Write down a positive affirmation for change. (*see examples in Chapter 7*)
5. Recite this affirmation every morning and evening for at least 21 days.
6. Journal every day for at least 21 days on how your life is changing positively.
7. Say a daily prayer of thanksgiving for life-sustaining change.

Many times a lack of change is not linked to fear, but to pride or a sense of entitlement to remain in the state of self-piety and its fog of false perfection. Prideful people cannot recognize their flaws or weaknesses and therefore are not compelled to make changes that reflect an internal evaluation of growth and maturity.

The scriptures state that, *"pride goes before destruction, a haughty spirit before a fall."* Proverbs 16:18 NIV In other words, one's short-sightedness or lack of clear perspective in regard to his or her need to change, ultimately ends in self-degradation. Our willingness to make changes in our thoughts, speech, attitude, and demeanor is a direct reflection of our personal maturation process and/or maturity level.

My father often repeated to my sister and me, *"every time you point at someone else, you have 3 more fingers pointing back at yourself."* It is always easier to see the changes that need to be made in others than it is to admit the changes we need to make within ourselves.

So, how do we move from infancy to adulthood in the area of change? First, we must admit that no one on this earth is perfect...including you. The scriptures declare that the only one who changes NOT is God. Admitting our faults and weaknesses is the first step onto the road of change. This road to change is characterized by humility, honesty, self-control, and faithfulness. All of this leads to the destination of sustained change in life.

Attitude
Courage
Toward
Instruction
Opportunity
Necessity

Our desire to change and become all that God wants us to be requires us to seek the Holy Spirit for His guidance, wisdom, and internal refreshing. Once we are renewed and transformed in our thought-life (mind), we can begin to meditate on God's word (Bible) and speak the promises of God over our lives. You cannot simply change your mind, actions, or desires simply by wishing it so. You have to make a conscious decision to surrender your ways unto the Lord and trust Him to make the changes in you and through you.

You have to take it a step further not just by praying for change, but also by having a heart of expectation and walking out by faith day by day in obedience to the direction and plan God has for your life.

Habitual change leads to a lifestyle of change. Take steps toward an effective lifestyle of change by adopting and executing the 4 Ps of Change.

4 "P"s of HABITUAL CHANGE

1. PURPOSE
2. PLAN
3. PRACTICE
4. PROGRESS

Real, life-altering (life-sustaining) change requires passion.

1. **PURPOSE** – Purpose is your God-given aim in life, your reason for living. Life with an objective for making an impact on society; creating a positive difference in the environment around you.

How do you know what your purpose is? It is something that has been a part of you all of your life that you have been uniquely created to perform on this earth. Not a career or job function. Not a means for *doing*, but a sense of *being*. Life's changes develop you, shape you, and direct you toward fulfilling your life's purpose.

A desire to live your life *on purpose* inevitably leads to the necessity for change in various areas of our lives.

2. **PLAN** - Have you found yourself longing for change, desiring change, but nothing seems to, well…change? Is it because your feet forgot to take you where your thoughts say you want to go? Our basic human nature continually yearns for newness and refreshing, but we want it to happen by osmosis.

In order to have "real," lifelong change, you have to take ACTION! Action requires planning. Planning requires strategy. Strategy requires ideas. Ideas require a "passion for change."

Let's define an action plan as a set of steps that define movement with a purpose and goal in mind. There are several steps to ensure that your plan towards change is beneficial and long lasting:

- ✓ 1st STEP: Examine your strength and weaknesses in the areas of relationship with self, relationship with others, socially, economically, and physically.
- ✓ 2nd STEP: Identify 1-2 weaknesses within each area listed in Step 1 that you would like to change.
- ✓ 3rd STEP: Create an objective and goal to effect change for those weaknesses.

You have heard the saying, *walk the talk.* We can sing a *"Change is going to Come"*, but real change does not take place until you make a conscious decision that you are sick and tired of being sick and tired.

3. **PRACTICE** – Once you are determined to walk out your purpose and define your plan, it takes practice to learn how to create a lifestyle of embracing life's changes in a positive manner.

Sometimes I feel like I am reliving the same situation over and over again. Do you ever feel that way? I have come to realize that when God is trying to perfect a certain area of my life He will send the same test over and over again. It may involve a new environment or different people, but the impact of the scenario is familiar.

In order to grow and achieve higher levels of aptitude, skill, and ability in a particular area, it requires experience and experience requires practical awareness and exposure to relevant changes in your life. We may think we have overcome a particular obstacle in our life, like fear or worry, until the next situation occurs. How we handle a situation on a continuous basis provides us the real life practice in developing new attitudes and reactions to the changes in our lives.

4. **PROGRESS** - Just like an Olympic athlete, as you dedicate time to practicing new habits for effectual change, you expect to see progress. It is imperative to establish measures that clearly monitor progress. As you progress, you expect to move forward in areas you commit to change. Do understand that sometimes you may experience temporary setbacks in your effort to implement lifelong change. Just remember that it is only temporary.

As you travel down the pathway of life, your journey will indeed be redirected by some course corrections. A detour does not mean that there is not an alternate path to reaching the same destiny. What appear to be failures or mistakes are all part of the ultimate plan to prepare you for your life's purpose.

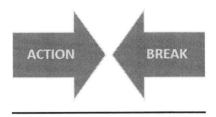

21-Days to Lifestyle Change

Studies indicate that sustained habits and lasting change require at least 21 days of repeatable, sustained behavior. Therefore, to effectively implement the 4 Ps of Change I suggest that you perform the outlined steps below over a 3-week period (7 days per week for 3 weeks = 21 days).

- ✓ Step 1: Identify Areas for Change
- ✓ Step 2: Develop, Plan & Document Purpose for Change
- ✓ Step 3: Commit to Change

Visit **www.BestLifeOnPurposeNow.com** for a copy of the **21-Days to Lifestyle Change** template.

Chapter 6

WRITE THE VISION AND MAKE IT PLAIN

"Vision without action is a Daydream. Action without vision is a Nightmare."
Japanese Proverb

Vision is an image of the future you seek to create. Vision is the ability to see beyond what is happening in your life today. Vision is the pathway to your destiny, while goals are the stepping stones that guide you down the path toward your vision.

In the Bible, Proverbs 29:18a states *"Where there is no vision, the people perish..."* People often live their lives aimlessly. They just drift minute by minute, hour by hour, day by day, and year after year with no clear focus for their lives and their future. If you are one of these people, today is the day to begin again. So, from where does vision come? God has ordained a purpose and plan for each of us. To tap into God's vision for your life, you have to get quiet and intentional.

Being intentional means a conscious decision to make things happen on purpose. I made a decision that I want to live my BEST life on purpose **now**. To understand the vision for my life, I prayed and asked God to direct me through the word of God and speak to my heart and mind in order to impart His vision for my life. Now I know you may say that God doesn't speak to you that way. But, the truth is that God will speak to you in a way that will get your attention. It may be through someone else's testimony, a song, a class, a friend, or maybe even a book. You have to decide to *stop, look,* and *listen.*

To help you in determining your vision, let us explore the characteristics associated with the word **"VISION"**:

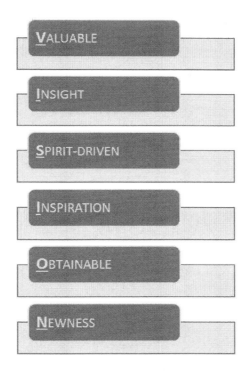

VALUABLE

INSIGHT

SPIRIT-DRIVEN

INSPIRATION

OBTAINABLE

NEWNESS

Do you know that your life is **Valuable** to God? When something or someone is deemed valuable it is because of a rare attribute that is not easily duplicated and has great worth. You are "one of a kind." God has a specific vison for your life. Examine yourself to identify your unique gifts, talents, and personality. In a world of copycats, you were called to be different...to simply be YOU.

In order to live out the vision God has for your life, you have to obtain **Insight**. Insight is the capacity to gain accurate and deep intuitive understanding of a person or thing. This requires quiet and focused prayer. Ask your heavenly Father why on earth you have been birthed at such a time as this.

When God told Moses to lead the children of Israel out of Egypt, Moses pleaded for God to teach him the way to go. Moses knew that he could not free the people without clear **Insight** from God for direction.

Moses said to the LORD, "You have been telling me, 'Lead these people,' but you have not let me know whom you will send with me. You have said, 'I know you by name and you have found favor with me.' If you are pleased with me, teach me your ways so I may know you and continue to find favor with you. Remember that this nation is your people." The LORD replied, "My Presence will go with you, and I will give you rest." Exodus 33:12-14

You may not always understand the complete picture, but God will give you each step along the way of your life's journey. He is waiting for you to take the first step which is simply to *ASK*.

You will be tempted to lead your life on your own and make decisions according to how you feel or what you believe to be right. But, remember vision is **Spirit-driven**. We must learn to submit our soul (mind, will, and emotions) to God's divine order. Please know that submission is not a bad word. It simply means to trust and follow the wisdom, guidance, and direction of the Lord because He loves and cares about your well-being.

"I thought, 'Age should speak;
advanced years should teach wisdom.'
But it is the spirit in a person,
the breath of the Almighty that gives them
understanding." Job 32:7-8 NIV

Knowing the vision for your life brings **Inspiration**. You are less likely to live your life like a deer in the headlights. Inspiration is the process of being mentally stimulated to do or feel something especially creative or innovative. Your vision inspires you to be better and do better.

"Behold, the LORD your God has set the land before
you; go up and take possession of it, just as the
LORD, the God of your fathers, has spoken to you.
Do not fear or be dismayed."
Deuteronomy 1:21 AMP

Do not be dismayed. The vision for your life is **Obtainable**. You have the ability to acquire or secure the purpose and plan God has for your life with His divine Inspiration. It is important not to copy someone else's vision. Yours is specific and unique for the gifts and abilities you possess.

When you have vision and walk out the vision for your life, there is a sense of **Newness** and renewal. You have to take the action steps necessary to bring the vision to pass. I dare you to write the vision and make it plain. See your life begin again.

"So here's what I want you to do, God helping you: Take your everyday, ordinary life—your sleeping, eating, going-to-work, and walking-around life—and place it before God as an offering. Embracing what God does for you is the best thing you can do for him. Don't become so well-adjusted to your culture that you fit into it without even thinking. Instead, fix your attention on God. You'll be changed from the inside out. Readily recognize what he wants from you, and quickly respond to it. Unlike the culture around you, always dragging you down to its level of immaturity, God brings the best out of you, develops well-formed maturity in you."
Romans 12:2 MSG

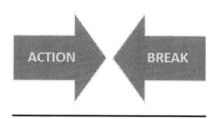

A vision statement is an image of the future you seek to create. The vision statement should be short and broad. You are defining what you want your life to look like without any consideration of the how. An example of a vision statement is:

"To live my BEST life on purpose."

You may have multiple vision statements for various areas of your life in addition to your overall life. These areas may include: family, spiritual development, health, and/or finances. Your vision should stretch you beyond what you perceive you can achieve based upon where you are today.

> *"Write the **Vision**, and make it plain upon tablets, that he may run that reads it"*

Visit **www.BestLifeOnPurposeNow.com** for a copy of the **Vision Statement** template.

Goals provide the specifics for achieving your vision. I know that many of us do not grasp the importance of defining and writing goals down on paper, but if you don't you inevitably walk aimlessly in life. To take your vision one step further. Develop **SMART** goals that support the vision statement(s) you have written for each area of your life. Goals should be **S**pecific, **M**easurable, **A**ttainable, **R**ealistic, and **T**ime-bound. Short-term goals are typically those life-milestones you want to achieve in the next 1-3 years, while long-term are usually more than 3 years away.

Take the challenge today to begin again and try something new. Take out a journal, notebook, or pad of paper and write your vision statement(s) and set goals for the following:

1. What are your top 3 goals in one or more of the following areas?

- ❖ Spiritual growth?
- ❖ Career or business?
- ❖ Family and friend relationships?
- ❖ Healthy lifestyle?

2. List 3 perceived obstacles that are keeping you from achieving your goals.

3. What are 3 steps you plan to take today to move forward in achieving your goals?

Chapter 7

AFFIRMATIONS FOR TRANSFORMATION

"Everybody is a genius. But, if you judge a fish by its ability to climb a tree, it will live its whole life believing that it is stupid."
Albert Einstein

30-Days of Affirmations for Transformation

DAY	TRANSFORMATION AFFIRMATION
1	"Your answer to change is a decision."
2	"Tomorrow comes even if you aren't ready."
3	"Change your thoughts and you change your perception; change your perception and you change your level of expectation."
4	"The success of my tomorrow is linked to my desire and decisions to change today."
5	"Today is the first day of the BEST days of my life!"
6	"Change doesn't always come easy, but the reward is so much sweeter down the road."
7	"My next triumph is only one decision away."
8	"To do differently, I must be different, to be different, I must think differently, to think differently, I must change my mindset (thoughts)."
9	"If I change my focus, I change me…for the better."
10	"Talk is cheap, but action is rewarding."
11	"Today's obstacles are tomorrow's opportunities to be an over comer."
12	"I am who I say I am."
13	"I have been created to do great things."
14	"I am one decision away from being the BEST me."
15	"I am an overcomer by the profession of my faith."
16	"I am a doer, not just a talker."

DAY	TRANSFORMATION AFFIRMATION
17	"I am moving forward regardless of my past."
18	"Stop, look, listen…act and do it again."
19	"I am running this race called life with excellence and determination."
20	"I trust that promises of my future are more than the lies of my past."
21	"I will begin again with or without fear."
22	"I will do it anyway."
23	"As the sun rises and sets in the east and the west, I will have the courage to get back up again."
24	"With every twist and turn, I will continue to stretch forward."
25	"I trust in the promises of God for my life more than the fear of the unknown."
26	"I may not be perfect, but I am full of possibilities."
27	"Today's decisions lead to tomorrow's victories."
28	"If I believe it I can achieve it."
29	"God has a supernatural purpose and plan for my life that I am ready to receive with faith."
30	"I am able to overcome life's challenges like an eagle that soars above a raging storm."

Scriptures for Transformation

❖ *"For as he thinks in his heart, so is he."* Proverbs 23:7 NKJV

❖ *"I can do all things through Christ who strengthens me."* Philippians 4:13 NKVJ

❖ *"For God has not given us the spirit of fear, but of power, and of love, and of a sound mind."* 2 Timothy 1:7 KJV

❖ *"Create in me a clean heart, O God; and renew a right spirit within me.* Psalm 51:10 KJV

❖ *"May these words of my mouth and this meditation of my heart be pleasing in your sight, Lord, my Rock and my Redeemer."* Psalm 19:14 NIV

❖ *"For as the body without the spirit is dead, so faith without works is dead also."* James 2:26 KJV

❖ *"Jesus Christ is the same yesterday, today, and forever."* Hebrews 13:8 KJV

❖ *"No, in all these things we are more than conquerors through him who loved us."* Romans 8:37 NIV

❖ *"The Lord will make you the head, not the tail. If you pay attention to the commands of the Lord your God that I give you this day and carefully follow them, you will always be at the top, never at the bottom."* Deuteronomy 28:13 NIV

❖ *"...If God is for us, who can be against us?"* Romans 8:31 NIV

❖ *"For it is God who works in you to will and to act in order to fulfill his good purpose."* Philippians 2:13 NIV

The Serenity Prayer

GOD, grant me the serenity
to accept the things
I cannot change,

Courage to change the
things I can, and the
wisdom to know the difference.

Living one day at a time;
Enjoying one moment at a time;
Accepting hardship as the
pathway to peace.

Taking, as He did, this
sinful world as it is,
not as I would have it.

Trusting that He will make
all things right if I
surrender to His Will;

That I may be reasonably happy
in this life, and supremely
happy with Him forever in
the next.

Amen

The full text of the original "Serenity Prayer" written by Reinhold
Niebuhr (1892-1971)

ABOUT THE AUTHOR

Nicole Moore Waddell is an award winning
Consultant, Transformational Life Coach, Speaker,
and Author. Ms. Waddell has been recognized as a
regional Top 100 MBE and has been featured in the
Daily Record and the Baltimore magazine as a
Woman Leader in Business. As a change agent, her
passion is to support others in their quest to live their
"Best Life on Purpose Now."

CONTACT US

To schedule author appearances for book signings, speaking engagements, coaching sessions or to attend our webinars, please visit us at:

www.BestLifeOnPurposeNow.com

<u>Or</u>

Email us at:
info@nicolemoorewaddell.com

Best Life On Purpose Now

A Virtual Link, LLC affiliate